Trouble-Free Transitions for New Teachers

Published in the United States of America
by Rowman & Littlefield Education
A Division of Rowman & Littlefield Publishers, Inc.
A wholly owned subsidiary of The Rowman & Littlefield
Publishing Group, Inc.
4501 Forbes Boulevard, Suite 200, Lanham, Maryland 20706
www.rowmaneducation.com

PO Box 317
Oxford
OX2 9RU, UK

British Library Cataloguing in Publication Information Available

Library of Congress Cataloging-in-Publication Data

Strike, Kimberly T., 1966–
  Trouble-free transitions for new teachers : elementary level /
Kimberly T. Strike.
     p. cm.
  Includes bibliographical references.
  ISBN-13: 978-1-57886-411-9 (pbk. : alk. paper)
  ISBN-10: 1-57886-411-9 (pbk. : alk. paper)
  1. First year teachers—Handbooks, manuals, etc. 2. Elementary
school teaching—Handbooks, manuals, etc. I. Title.
  LB2844.1.N4.S82 2006
  372.11—dc22   2006012680

♾ ™ The paper used in this publication meets the minimum
requirements of American National Standard for Information
Sciences—Permanence of Paper for Printed Library Materials,
ANSI/NISO Z39.48-1992.
Manufactured in the United States of America.

A special thank you to my husband, Jeffrey; my children: James, Jared, and ElizabethAnne; my dad, Ed; and to Joan, my best friend and mom, who titled the book and has always encouraged and supported me. Each of you has played a special role in my life, now reflected in my writing. I love you!

Contents

Acknowledgments

This handbook was developed specifically for the first-year teacher or new building transfer. The idea and format for this project is based on a handbook I received as a new teacher from the Wisconsin Education Association Council's (WEAC) Instruction and Professional Development Committee (IPD): *The Beginning Teacher Handbook: A Book of Firsts* (1989). After teaching for ten years, I went into school administration and still found myself referring back to the handbook as I worked with my own faculty. I began to add, delete, and modify based on the needs of my faculty and the specific building in which I served. As I began working with student teachers, candidates for alternative licensure, and students in upper-level coursework through CESA and local universities, I identified three main areas that were challenging to new teachers: time management, classroom management, and lesson planning. The document before you is a culmination of

WEAC's beginning teacher handbook, additional resources, and years of experience in working with new and pre-service teachers to pinpoint areas that are challenging and to provide assistance or resources before the challenges became problematic. It has been cross-referenced with information from teachers new to the field between 2000 and 2004, with the assistance of Dr. William Henk (dean of Marquette University's School of Education) and Dr. James Juergensen (dean of Concordia University of Wisconsin's School of Education). Thank you to the educators who took the time to candidly answer questions and thoughtfully reflect upon their new placement in the field. The information shared will enhance the art and science of teaching, make the transition to teaching (or teaching in a new building) easier, and provide a successful experience for teachers, their colleagues, and the children whose lives they touch.

Introduction

Welcome! You have joined a dynamic, dedicated
group of professionals. As you read through this book,
many questions will arise. Feel free to bring these
questions to your principal, your assigned mentor, or
any staff member—since educators recognize the importance of and operate as a team. Your challenge is to
engage your students while teaching the assigned curriculum and to assist each student in reaching his or
her potential. In the words of Sidney Hook, "Everyone
who remembers his own educational experience remembers teachers, not methods and techniques." Now
the opportunity to help shape the future lies within
you.

Cura personalis: care for the person. Let no one fall
between the cracks.

Chapter One

What New Teachers Need to Know

OVERVIEW OF THE SCHOOL

Every school has a culture of its own, even if it's part of a larger district. It's important to gain an understanding of the school and the district in which you'll work, as well as your role as an educator within that district. To better understand your district, you should find out about the following:

- The school district or central governing agency of your school, the policymakers, hiring agent/s, and overall chain of command. Get to know them by name and position, and gain an understanding of district protocol.
- The people who prepare, present, and report on the budget, and those who determine budget cuts.
- Area economics.
- New developments and subdivisions in your district.
- Demographics of your school.

- Current enrollment and recent trends.
- Educational and extracurricular programs in your school.
- Your school's open enrollment plan, if any.
- The number of faculty members, support staff, and administrators.
- Points of interest about the school.
- Specific instructional methods used district- and schoolwide.
- Areas of recognition for the school, personnel, or students.
- Areas identified for improvement within the school.
- Parental involvement within the school.
- Schoolwide activities that parents and students anticipate.
- The issues currently facing this particular school and district, and the plan (both short-term and long-term) to handle them. How will your role as an educator fit in to this plan?
- If and how early childhood students are separated from older students, for example: Is there a separate wing for early childhood classrooms? Do younger students follow a different schedule, including recesses? Do students attend a half day or full day? Do half-day students eat lunch at school?

WHY THIS BOOK?

Your initial year of teaching will be filled with transition: a new building, a new boss, new colleagues, new students and families, new rules, a new schedule and curriculum, and possibly even a new community.

The change from student to teacher can be simultaneously exciting and exhausting. It's said that it takes a person three years to learn a job and become familiar with both the available resources and required procedures. As reported by Heller (2004):

> A study published in the *American Educational Research Journal* and conducted by Richard M. Ingersoll, an associate professor of education and sociology at Philadelphia University, found the average yearly turnover rate in education is 13.2 percent as compared to 11 percent in other professions. Even more significant to the problem under discussion here is that 29 percent of new teachers leave education within their first three years, and by the end of five years, 39 percent have left (Viadero, 2002, p. 7). Ingersoll concludes that educators should spend less time on recruitment efforts and put more effort into retaining the teachers they have. . . . To make matters worse, the teachers who leave tend to be the best new recruits (Gordon and Maxey, 2000, p. 8). (p. 4–5)

The frustration that results from inexperience, isolation, and the lack of practical know-how can be overwhelming to the beginner. Keep in mind that your colleagues had to start somewhere; every one of them had a first year of teaching, and most will have tales to tell. Teaching is virtually the only profession where a beginner is fully responsible for all aspects of his or her profession from the first day and, in fact, is expected to perform the same tasks as an experienced professional. True "on the job" training.

Many times teachers feel isolated, but there is no need for that isolation. Early in your professional career, try to develop the perspective that teaching is a cooperative and collaborative undertaking. Be willing to ask questions and exchange ideas with your colleagues. Beginning teachers are often assigned a mentor teacher during their first year. This person is an experienced and effective teacher who communicates well and is willing to share knowledge and insights into the profession with you. This book is to be used in conjunction with your professional colleagues. It will assist in asking questions, finding answers, and generating discussion.

Your initial year of teaching presents many "firsts." For the first time you'll be on your own in a classroom. For the first time you might be asked to teach a student whose native language isn't English, to assign detentions, or to handle a fight on the playground. For the first time you might find yourself in a room of 28 students, nine of whom have special needs, with no aide assigned to you. This book has been designed to help you begin to anticipate some of these firsts. Having the opportunity to think or talk about some common situations before you actually encounter them can assist you when you actually have to handle that situation. In the words of Franklin Roosevelt, "Make the mistakes of yesterday your lessons for today."

BEFORE THE FIRST DAY OF SCHOOL

It isn't uncommon for educators to begin working long before that exciting first day of school when the children arrive. How you prepare for that first day can make a big difference in your success. Since the first day sets the tone, your approach and preparation will make a difference in how that first day, week, month, quarter, semester, and year of school will go for you in your new teaching position. A little time invested in advance will be beneficial in the long run.

Part of good teaching is finding the time to think about the things you do as a teacher. To help develop the habit of reflection, keep a daily journal where you can record the day's experiences; your thoughts on what went on in your classroom; and the questions, concerns, and ideas for teaching that you have each day. You'll be truly amazed at the growth you see in yourself when you reread the journal later. Another easy way to document your reflective teaching is within your lesson plans. Good teachers can usually identify what went well and what didn't go so well within a lesson. Documenting these observations within the plan will assist you when teaching that lesson, unit, or chapter in the future. This holds true for teacher-prepared as well as published material. For example, if your students were totally confused by directions on a worksheet, are you going to continue to use that worksheet as written or can you make adjustments in your teaching, the directions on the worksheet, or the assignment to make the worksheet less confusing? Better yet, question yourself: Does a worksheet reflect the best method of assessment or is there an alternative assessment you could use to avoid the confusion?

Each and every school is unique. Therefore, not all ideas listed here will apply to you and your new teaching position. Find out as much as you can about your school. Call the school and ask when you can stop in. Make note of the telephone number, fax number, and address of your school, then visit. While you are there, be sure to find:

- A map of the school showing fire exits and extinguishers, which should be posted in each classroom and visible to students.
- The main office.
- The principal's office.
- Your classroom.
- The library/learning resource center.
- Where audio-visual equipment and materials are housed, as well as the checkout or sign-up procedures.
- The healthroom. Question if there are extra clothes available should the need arise; if none are available through the school, begin a collection of your own (complete with plastic bags).
- Other rooms needed, such as the gymnasium or computer lab.

- Where your mailbox is located.
- The teachers' lounge, and faculty lunchroom.
- The faculty restroom.
- The faculty parking lot, student parking lot, and where to obtain a parking permit if necessary.
- A school calendar.
- Computers and software.
- Copy equipment, toner, and paper.
- The location of general supplies, the person to go to when supplies are low, and the procedure for ordering.
- Secretarial assistance.
- Student health information (allergies, seizures, diabetes, etc.).
- Lunchroom and meal purchase procedures for students. Are off-campus lunches allowed?
- Location of maintenance office. Get to know maintenance personnel by name and work shifts.
- Location and use of work orders.
- The schedules of colleagues who teach at your grade level, plus one year above and one year below. You should have excellent communication with these colleagues, and they can be an excellent resource.
- State and local requirements for your grade level.
- Procedures for locking down the school and where guests sign in. Does the school use visitor badges?
- Alarm/security information. Find out if hanging items from blinds or ceiling tiles will set off your security system, if cameras or codes are used, and what you need to know about them.

- Location and use of faculty forms.
- Location of the laminator and fax machines.
- What you need to know about the telephone system. Are there different rings? Are teachers expected to answer the telephone if office personnel are not able to do so? How do you transfer calls?
- Use of the public announcement or intercom system.

BE SURE TO FIND OUT

Prior to the start of the school year, get to know the professional expectations of your position. This will alleviate questions or tension in the future. Here are some recommendations:

- Obtain a copy of your contract. Know the terms and renewal process.
- Is there a probationary period in your contract?
- What are the requirements for tenure?
- Obtain copies of the faculty and family handbooks.
- Know what benefits you're entitled to and be sure to complete all necessary paperwork to participate in these benefits.
- Obtain a copy of the pay scale and pay schedule.
- Find out about various types of time off, such as sick, personal, professional, vacation, funeral, and jury duty. How are you expected to call these days in and to whom?
- What deductions (e.g., Social Security, insurance, and flex benefits) are taken from your pay?

- Learn about the retirement plan and how it works.
- Fill out the necessary forms the school requires to be included in your personnel file: application, resume, philosophy of teaching, transcripts, I-9, criminal background check (national check and fingerprints), contract, attendance, observations/evaluations, W2, insurance enrollment, flexible spending account enrollment, teaching license (or certification plan), physical examination (including drug test and TB test), and improvement plan (if necessary).
- Is there a teachers' union? How does the union work? Is membership required? Who is the union representative for your building, district, or area? How has the union assisted teachers in the past? How are relations between the teachers, union, and district? What do you need to know? Have contracts been issued on time? Have the teachers walked out or participated in movements to show dissatisfaction? What are the union's expectations of you as a new teacher?
- Does the district contribute toward your continued education?
- Who should you contact if there is a problem with your paycheck or benefits?
- Are there opportunities for stipends?
- Are faculty committees established? For what purpose(s)? How often do they meet?
- Learn about schedules and typical agendas for faculty/staff meetings.
- What are the contracted hours for teachers?

- What are the office hours of the school?
- Locate the curriculum for your grade level.
- Check the state standards and local benchmarks that you'll be responsible for in your new teaching placement.
- Where should you place outgoing mail?
- What's the homework policy?
- What's the school policy for students who miss work?
- Is homework given out early for vacations? Are report cards or progress reports issued early?
- What are the procedures for dealing with disciplinary problems?
- What's the school policy for referrals for special education, speech and language, gifted and talented, and Title I assistance?
- What's the policy on dispensing medication?
- What are the procedures for fire and tornado drills?
- What are the procedures for petty cash purchases?
- How is information communicated between the home and school, and between administration and staff?
- Make sure you have all the forms you'll need the first week of school, know what information should be included on each, and understand how they're handled (e.g., in reporting student absences or tardiness).
- Do students need to use hall passes for the restroom, library, or computer lab?

- What should you do in the event of teacher illness (who to contact and when, and how to provide lesson plans and materials for your substitute)?
- What are the summer school opportunities?
- Who's responsible for cleaning the teachers' lounge, microwave, refrigerator, etc.?
- What should you do in case of an emergency (security, medical, CPR, crisis intervention team, etc.)?
- Know the location of and how to complete progress reports.
- Know how to have an announcement read over the PA system.
- How do you sign up for the computer lab and media such as TV, VCR, or DVD?
- What supervisory duties, such as recess or bus, are you responsible for?
- What are the expectations for homeroom and the morning routine (e.g., the pledge of allegiance and announcements)?
- Are there special schedules to know about (e.g., shortened days for teacher in-service)?
- What is the dismissal procedure for students?
- Where should your lesson plans be kept for easy access by a substitute teacher? Are you required to turn in a copy? If so, to whom and when?
- What is the school grading policy (scale) and at what grade level does honor roll begin?
- What kind of celebrations does the school have for holidays, birthdays, or other events?

- How are deliveries made to students for items such as flowers or balloons?
- Are there spirit days?
- What is the assignment of lockers, cubbies, or other space to place personal items?
- Learn about the distribution of information to parents (office to parent or teacher to parent).
- Inquire as to what events are important to the school and to parents, particularly within your grade. That doesn't mean you *have* to do it, but be cognizant of what's important to the school community and decide if the event fits into the curriculum.
- Which extracurricular activity will you coordinate or supervise? Plan early.
- Is there a master calendar on which to place events such as assemblies, field trips, and extracurricular activities?

BE SURE TO MEET

- Your colleagues. They are an excellent resource, open and helpful. Meet colleagues who teach the same grade level, as well as one grade level above and below. See if staff members socialize outside of the school setting and participate as much as you can.
- Your mentor. Make a list of questions that you might need to ask this key person. Don't be hesitant to ask about things that are of concern to you. It's a good

idea to ask your mentor about in-service opportunities and to assist you in preparing for the beginning of school. Work with your mentor to develop what will probably be your first professional collaboration.

- The principal, the educational leader of the school. It's often helpful to ask the principal about his or her vision for the school or the atmosphere or school climate.
- Assistant principal(s). In many cases the assistant principal is responsible for discipline and scheduling.
- The secretary, the principal's right-hand person. This person is often the key to the everyday running of the school and is knowledgeable about finances, procedure, policy, supply orders, book orders, materials, and buses. The secretary is a great resource.
- Maintenance personnel. Get to know them by name and by shift. Use work orders as necessary. Find out the cleaning schedule: Are classrooms cleaned every day? How often are the floors mopped? Who is responsible for wiping desktops and how often is this done? How is recycling handled?
- Support personnel, e.g., the school nurse or educational assistants.
- Parent volunteers. What is the level of parental involvement and in what capacity do parents volunteer?
- School board members. Find out about elections, roles, members, subcommittees, and length of terms.

- PTA members. Find out about elections, duties, sub-committees, members, involvement in school functions, primary function, special events, fundraising participation, etc.

BE SURE TO HAVE

- Your schedule
- Lesson plans, with duties noted
- Curriculum guides for content in your assigned grade level or special area
- State standards and local benchmarks you are responsible for in your assigned placement
- Adequate numbers of copies of the textbooks you're using
- Family, faculty, and new teacher handbooks
- Your collective bargaining agreement
- Keys and security information
- Class lists
- Locker or cubby assignments
- Attendance forms and procedure
- Supplies ordered for your classroom: grade book or computer codes, lesson plan book, paper, pencils, pens, paper clips, rubber bands, masking tape, scotch tape, scissors, chalk, dry erase markers, stapler, and staples
- Your classroom budget
- Staff telephone numbers via emergency tree or faculty directory

- Information from the principal
- Completed personnel file
- Information and procedure on continuing education credits
- A staff-member "buddy" to eyeball notes home to the parents—an extra set of eyes can be very helpful

BE SURE YOU KNOW

Decide what you'll teach and do the first day of school: Make a detailed schedule, making sure to include time for each class, restroom breaks, lunch, student breaks, time for administrative paperwork, and a breather for yourself.

Write down everything, including what you plan to cover, procedures, and at what point you plan to do various activities. Plan at least twice as much as you think you'll have time to cover in a day. Plan several extra activities in case some or all of your students quickly complete scheduled activities. Try to provide work that all students can complete successfully and that you can correct and return the next day.

Know the curriculum and scope and sequence chart, and think about how you're going to teach the material. Review all lesson plans. Be sure to have materials prepared and copied in advance. You should also:

- Straighten your room and try to make it look inviting.

- Decorate the bulletin boards. All boards need to be covered. The board should change with seasons/events, with the exception of the calendar. Keep it simple and tasteful, but unusual and exciting. Over-stimulation or clutter will detract from learning.
- Arrange the desks and chairs, making sure that all desks have a clear visual path to the board, overhead, or other areas of the classroom that are used. Check your classroom information to see if preferential seating is necessary for any students.
- Copy, collect, and organize your materials. Be prepared: students know if you're organized and prepared or not. Don't wait until the morning of or class period before to do copying. Machinery isn't always dependable, particularly in humid weather.
- Familiarize yourself with attendance and lunch procedures.
- Think about the climate of your classroom, which will evolve as a direct result of your decisions as a teacher. Classroom rules of conduct should be clear and posted. It's much easier to loosen up as you go along than to try to tighten up after your students already have too much freedom. Be cognizant of teacher talk vs. student talk. Decide what you'll share about yourself with your students. Decide on the degree of formality in your teaching style.
- Know where forms are located.
- Demonstrate professionalism, including attire (no midriff shirts, miniskirts, or flip-flops, etc.). Learn

about your district and building guidelines regarding professional attire.
- Can teachers drink beverages while they teach, e.g., coffee, tea, or water? What about food or snacks?
- Can students drink beverages or eat snacks in the classroom?

WORK CITED

Heller, D. A. (2004). *Teachers Wanted: Attracting and Retaining Good Teachers*. Alexandria, VA: Association for Supervision and Curriculum Development.

Chapter Two

The School Year

AS THE SCHOOL YEAR APPROACHES

If you plan to drive to school each morning, drive it once during the time you would normally commute to school to find the best route and check traffic patterns and time. Place yourself on a "school training schedule" to get used to the hours. Subscribe to a local newspaper or view it online. Become familiar with local attitudes, ideas, and community values. Enjoy a short vacation, if possible. Complete or reschedule projects to alleviate stress once the school year begins. Get a large calendar for your desk and jot down important dates, upcoming events and commitments, and appointments. Get to know your community:

- Emergency telephone numbers
- Post office locations and zip codes

- Utility companies that serve you
- Recreation, exercise, and sports activities that are nearby
- Public library and Bookmobile
- Parks, zoos, museums, theater, historical sites, etc.
- Radio and television stations
- Universities and colleges
- Grocery stores, bookstores, shopping malls, and education supply stores
- Banking institutions: locations, telephone numbers, and hours
- Medical facilities
- Local parking regulations (snow dates, alternate parking, etc.)
- Dates for special events at the school (open house, concerts, talent show, etc.)

Check into collaborative efforts and partnerships between the school and local universities or businesses. For example, local universities might offer scholarships or reciprocal relationships to teachers. Establish a relationship with area businesses to upgrade computer equipment, and locate other organizations to whom you can donate your used equipment.

Create an introductory letter to parents letting them know who you are and what your expectations are. Include items such as homework, parental involvement, school supplies, appropriate dress for the weather, and birthday treats.

THE FIRST DAY

As you actually begin the practice of teaching, you might find the following suggestions to be helpful:

- Be visible to your students when they arrive and greet them prior to entering the classroom. The playground is a great place to begin.
- Assign seats or allow students to choose. Either way, make a seating chart so you can call on students by name during the period.
- Set expectations with students for students.
- Review the specific rules for behavior along with their consequences and rewards and do so in a non-threatening way. Be firm but fair. Maintain discipline. It is recommended to post no more than five classroom rules.
- If you give a homework assignment the first night, make it one that your students can be successful doing and one you can correct and return the next day.
- Check your mailbox every day, several times if possible. Messages are left throughout the day. The intercom system or telephones should be used only when deemed necessary to minimize classroom disruption.
- Use pencil the first week or two, as changes are common.
- Plan to arrive at school early and stay late at least for the first few weeks. Teaching during this period is likely to be tiring, so keep personal commitments to a

minimum. Be prepared to be very tired for a few weeks.

- Clarify your homework policy.
- Realize that there will be many forms and much paperwork to do. Don't let it overwhelm you.
- Have a list of supplies you want your students to purchase. These are typically distributed to families in the spring and then again in the fall.
- Recognize that you don't know everything and that you don't *need* to know everything. Be willing to ask questions and eager to collaborate with your colleagues.
- Always escort your class to and from specialists, assemblies, lunch, etc.
- Check your school's policy on water, snack, and restroom breaks.

THE FIRST WEEK

- Get to know your colleagues. Get in the habit of exchanging ideas and professional insights.
- Get to know the special education resources and referral process.
- Get to know resources available, including library, computer, etc.
- Identify student health problems. Note any possible hearing or vision problems for preferential seating and parent contact. Decide what to do in case of a medical emergency.

- Familiarize yourself with procedures for student tardiness or truancy.
- Familiarize yourself with local procedures for student abuse or neglect.
- Locate accessible telephones. Check local policies on cell phones for both teachers and students.
- Know who's in charge when the principal is out of the building.
- Keep accurate records of attendance, behavior, assignments, and fee collection.
- Prepare a substitute folder.
- Learn students' names as quickly as possible. They appreciate it and respond better when addressed by name.
- Keep a professional journal. Record daily questions, thoughts, and impressions about your teaching. Consider what worked, what didn't work, and why. Consider what sort of student responses occurred in class. Consider which students were successful that day, which weren't, and possible reasons. Review and reflection are the first steps in individual professional growth and development. When reading your journal, you'll recognize the journey you've endured, see your growth, and have something tangible to turn back to when entering year two.

THE FIRST MONTH

- Know when regular meetings are planned (staff, school board, PTA, faculty committees, etc.).

- Know the policy and procedure for scheduling field trips, collecting money, and ordering transportation.
- Know the location of student files.
- Know the procedure and dates for sending out student progress reports.
- Know the procedures for assemblies.
- Find out your district's policy on attending teachers' conventions. Is it a contracted day? Is attendance mandatory or optional?
- Get to know the overall makeup of the student body.
- Get to know your colleagues. Make an effort to do things with other teachers.
- Get involved in school activities.
- It's usually about this time that the daily needs of the teaching profession begin to overwhelm the beginning teacher, corresponding with a decline in enthusiasm and fading of idealism. Be cognizant of this and don't let it happen. Your enthusiasm for students and your idealism about what teachers can do is vital. Preserve them! Remember that you aren't alone. Discuss your feelings with colleagues. Collaborate, communicate, and cooperate with them to accomplish your common goal of providing a quality education for the students and assisting each student in reaching his or her potential.

THE FIRST QUARTER

- Get to know the various student organizations, clubs, and teams.

- Attend a school activity voluntarily. This can mean a great deal to parents and students alike.
- Know the procedure for identifying students who need assistance and referring them to the public school system for special education.
- Know the resources for gifted and talented students.
- Become familiar with other special programs that are unique to your school, and make contact with the people who are associated with them.
- Find out where to obtain information on school closings and what obligations you have.
- Learn how to fill out report cards and where to document state standards and local benchmarks.
- Familiarize yourself with areas such as grading, retention, behavioral issues, and graduations (preschool, kindergarten, and those moving on to middle school).

THE FIRST SEMESTER

- Get to know budgeting procedures and cycles.
- Get to know the procedure for determining need, placing, and recording an order.
- Know the procedures for using media in the classroom. Can you sign up for library or computer use outside of specialist class time? How do you sign up for televisions, VCRs, DVDs, or a projector? What ratings are acceptable in your district? Do you need parental permission for media? What media are available, e.g., filmstrips and movies? Do you have

other resources available, such as a local public library or a school in another district? What is the reason for choosing media? How will the media effectively tie into your curriculum? Will it enhance classroom discussion before and after a lesson? Will it inspire student writing or intrigue students to learn more about a topic? Will you use it to compare a novel to a movie? Do you need to show the whole video or just a segment to get your point across? Did you preview the video to ensure it's at the appropriate age or grade level? Did you test the equipment to be sure it works? Is there a glare on the screen? Is the quality of the tape okay? How is the volume? How will you promote active participation, e.g., study guides, questions, note taking, problem solving, alternative endings or letters to a character, author, or film director?

• Get to know free material resources.

Chapter Three

Professional Aspects

SETTING GOALS

It's imperative for teachers to set goals. Goal setting allows them to improve the quality of their teaching. Although the process might seem complex and demanding, it's necessary in order to create excellence in education.

Goals are directly tied to the teaching standards that identify benchmarks of effective teaching. The wording of the goals should reflect the "knowledge, skills, and dispositions" (KSD) tied to the teaching standards. By using the KSD as a guide, pre-service teachers gain an understanding of the standards and what they need to attain, while new teachers have documentation readily available to keep in mind their direction, goals, continual assessment, and reflective practice.

Through the process of setting goals, individual teachers take into account the community in which they teach as well as the culture of the school and the individuality of the students, and then they adapt their knowledge to ensure effective student learning.

The goals that are chosen need to be measurable. Teachers must determine the type of evaluation and assessment they believe will best demonstrate improvement. With student teachers, evaluation and assessment that demonstrates attainment of goals is the case more often than not.

You must move beyond collection of data to understand effective teaching and student learning, and meeting the needs of students. Reflect on where you are as an educator and set your goals based on where you want to or need to go.

Goals reflect both long- and short-range plans for professional growth and development. Although the enhancement of teaching skills is recognized as a life-long process, goals define the planned areas of focus for a predetermined timeline. For example, if a student teacher is in a triplacement due for early childhood licensure, the goals would change to be specific to each of the three individual placements. As a new teacher entering the field of education, your goals might break down by quarter, semester, or school year.

The number of goals set should be a workable number, and the goals as written should be attainable within the time frame. Be careful to challenge yourself without frustrating or setting yourself up for failure.

Seek guidance and support to achieve success in reaching or even surpassing your goals.

MAINTAINING PROFESSIONALISM

Teaching is a profession. Other professionals in the field, as well as those outside the field such as parents or lawmakers, have certain expectations of teachers. People often believe that earning a degree means they've earned professional status, but being a professional goes beyond earning a degree. While there are several meanings of the word, *professionalism* in the context I'm using refers to having the qualifications of a particular profession and being well-trained, good at what you do, and dependable. Therefore, merely doing a job for a certain number of years doesn't make you a professional, nor does having acquired a particular degree. Certain characteristics are necessary for professionalism, including:

- Being a role model: character, integrity, honesty, forthrightness, trustworthiness
- Being a reflective practitioner and striving for continual improvement
- Being responsible and accountable
- Projecting a professional image, including attire and appropriate language
- Displaying professional maturity and conduct
- Maintaining confidences and confidentiality

- Being willing to take direction and follow instruction
- Accepting your current place in a system and following protocol or chain of command in working within that system
- Addressing others by title
- Being a team player
- Demonstrating respect to students, parents, school board members, administrators, etc.
- Being loyal to your organization and co-workers, e.g., honoring and not abusing contractual issues
- Doing what's right
- Planning
- Making decisions
- Communicating openly and appropriately
- Pressing for excellence
- Doing your job to the best of your ability without constant direction and without excuses

Remember that your students and school families see you in the community, such as at the grocery store, church, or a local restaurant, as well as in the school setting. You've chosen a career in which you're a public servant. As such, you live your life in a fishbowl for all to see, and your personal life will be public.

LEGAL ISSUES

From calling grades aloud in class to searching lockers, the education system has come under fire and been challenged through the legal system. Many unions and districts offer legal services to members or employees. Ask about your legal benefits.

Following is a list of some policies you want to check into prior to the students' attendance. Though not a comprehensive list, it will give you an idea of some issues you might face as an educator:

- Due process
- Prior notice of expectations
- Notification of penalty applied
- Notification of charges against student
- Allowing student to respond
- Providing a hearing to ensure a fair decision
- Providing equal opportunities for students regardless of race, religion, sexual orientation, gender, socio-economic status, handicap/s, behavior, etc.
- Choice of classroom management strategies:
  - Corporal punishment
  - Time out
  - Detentions and suspensions
  - Homework policies
  - Dress codes and uniforms
  - Participation in and suspension from extracurricular activities
  - Participation in and suspension from field trips
  - Search and seizure (e.g., lockers, cars, backpacks, and purses)
  - Fights
  - Language, threats, and bullying

- Weapons
- "No tolerance" policies

A TIME FOR REFLECTION

Reflective teaching goes hand-in-hand with effective planning and execution of lessons. Unfortunately, a high number of demands require prioritizing within limited time allotments, and these demands often outweigh reflection on past practice. Yet it's important for teachers—all teachers—to realize the importance of reflection because it's open, honest reflection that allows us to identify our successes, failures, strengths, weaknesses, and changes we still need to make. Good teachers will tell you that they've had lessons that didn't go as planned. Some teachers will even find humor in lessons that "bombed." Reflection and change are components of good teaching.

The questions listed below are designed to help you focus your thinking on past professional practice. They're designed to develop the habit of professional thoughtfulness and personal evaluation and to stimulate a search for more effective teaching practices. You can use your response to these questions as journal entries or to stimulate collaborative discussion with your mentor or other colleagues:

- What kinds of questions have you been asking during classroom discussions or on your exams? Do those questions stimulate thinking and creativity as well as recall? Do some of your questions have a variety of appropriate answers?

- What's the rate of student success in your classroom? What about student failure? What kinds of students tend to succeed? Which ones fail? Is there a pattern?
- Do you think students enjoy coming to your classroom to learn? What are the conditions that appear to contribute to the atmosphere of joyful learning? How can those conditions be enhanced in your classroom?
- What is your relationship with the parents of your students? Have you developed any mutual problem-solving relationships? How many parents have you contacted with a "good news" message?
- Do you have a "professional best friend"? Have you invited this colleague to watch you teach? Have you watched your colleague teach? Do you have time committed to a discussion of professional matters?
- Do students leave your classroom open to future learning?
- What professional journal are you now reading regularly? What is its appeal?
- How do you respond to the range of student abilities in your classroom? Do you ask students to learn alone? Do you ask them to help each other learn? What lessons have you planned to facilitate cooperative learning?
- What do you think about the content you teach? Is it something external that students must absorb? Are

meanings "out there" waiting to be internalized? Do students create a meaning in your classroom? When do they do that?

- Most learning is hard work and requires student engagement for it to occur at an optimal level. Engagement can be inferred from the time students are willing to spend on academic tasks, the intensity of their concentration, their enthusiasm, and the care with which they complete their tasks. Are your students engaged?

Following are some prompts for your professional journal:

- As the school year begins, I'm most nervous or anxious about . . .
- As the school year begins, I'm most excited about . . .
- I encouraged my students to think critically when . . .
- I encouraged my students to problem-solve when . . .
- I engaged my students in the lesson by . . .
- I saw how excited my students were when . . .
- I could improve that lesson by . . .
- I need to contact . . .
- My most challenging student . . .
- Something I learned from my students is . . .
- I wish my students would . . .
- I wish my district would . . .
- I can affect my students' lives by . . .
- My students affect my life by . . .
- My favorite lesson this week was . . .

- My students really enjoyed . . .
- I felt overwhelmed when . . .
- I remembered to praise my students when . . .
- My most creative lesson has been . . .
- What I need to focus on is . . .
- I know my students are learning because . . .
- Some great questions my students have asked are . . .
- I felt uncomfortable when . . .
- I am glad I went into teaching because . . .

INDUCTION ACTIVITIES

Unanticipated events will occur. Be flexible and adaptable in responding to the unexpected. Ask your mentor for suggestions on how to deal with situations such as:

- A child becoming ill
- A student who has a health concern, e.g., diabetes, asthma, or allergies
- A student crying
- Inclement weather causing indoor recess
- Dealing with death (relative, friend, or pet)
- A student wetting him- or herself
- A parent who's angry or unreasonable
- A student refusing to do what you asked of him or her
- A student falling asleep in class
- Being called by the office during a class
- Non-English-speaking students being assigned to your class

- Saying or doing something embarrassing in front of the class
- A fight breaking out and you're the nearest faculty member
- Suspecting substance abuse by a student or colleague

In addition to considering questions such as these, it's strongly recommended that the beginning teacher have regularly planned discussions with his or her mentor. Collaboration and professional discussion are key to professional growth and development. Topics of discussion could include (items followed by an asterisk are addressed in more detail in chapter 1):

1. Classroom management*
   - Heading off inappropriate behavior*
   - Classroom rules*
   - Student behavior
   - Listening
   - Student motivation
   - Reward systems for students
   - Policies for planned absence and make-up work
2. Time management*
   - Overall planning
   - Specific lessons and transition periods
   - Balancing personal and professional duties without becoming overwhelmed
3. Planning effective lessons*
   - Components of an effective lesson*

4. Instructional strategies*
   - Choosing the best instructional strategy for a lesson, objective, or assessment with a particular group of students*
5. Discipline procedures
   - Detention (when is it held, what do they do, how long is it?)
   - Uniform or dress code (what to do when a student shows up out of uniform/dress code, consequences, warm weather dress)
6. Bullying
   - Addressing the situation
   - Not turning a deaf ear
   - Identifying the students at fault and the consequence earned
   - Deciding if the parent(s) or principal need to be notified
7. Evaluating student performance
   - Consistent with school grading scale
   - Record keeping
   - Filling out a report card or progress report
   - Parent–teacher–student conferences*
   - Different forms of evaluation
   - Parent–teacher communication*
8. Multicultural awareness
   - Bilingual/bicultural resources
   - Appropriate teaching techniques to help the child
   - Language abilities: monolingual/bilingual, language spoken in the home
   - Cultural diversity

9. Teaching styles
    - Development of your own teaching style*
    - Professional classroom demeanor*
    - Classroom strategies
    - Developing communication skills
    - Using community resources
    - Learning styles: both yours and the students'
    - Teaching techniques, e.g., cooperative learning and differentiated instruction
10. Supervision and evaluation
    - Clinical and standards-based supervision
    - Being observed and supervised: new teachers are observed four times throughout the year and veteran staff members are observed only once
    - Confidentiality and evaluation
    - Expectations for the beginning teacher
11. Professional growth and development opportunities
    - Professional organizations in your discipline or area of special interest
    - Upcoming conferences, workshops, and policies that pertain to your attendance
12. Special education
    - Names of students
    - Resources
    - Instructional strategies
    - Appropriate materials
    - Modification
    - Use of the learning resource center (LRC)

13. Technology in the classroom
   - Acceptable use policy (AUP)
   - Technology integration such as VHS, DVD, CDs, Internet searches, bookmarking sites, Power Point presentations, and political cartoons
   - Inappropriate use has consequences: be in tune with the sites your students are visiting and games they're playing
   - Virus protection
   - E-mail use by students
   - E-mail use by faculty

Chapter Four

Connecting the Classroom to the Real World

If you're wondering what's in store for you, you're in good company. The experiences of first-year teachers run the gamut, from those who have a wonderful experience to those who cry on a daily basis. Hopefully, experienced teachers will take new teachers under their wing and guide them in becoming excellent educators. This book cannot comprehensively answer every question or address every concern of a new teacher. So you can better understand some of the challenges you might face, this chapter provides the answers to a survey that was conducted with approximately 200 teachers (with an approximate 25% return rate) new to the field in 2000–2004. The survey asked the new teachers about topics such as difficulties they encountered in the school their first day, what information they needed as a new teacher, and what they considered to be the most important thing to know going into the job.

QUESTIONS FOR A NEW
ELEMENTARY TEACHER TO ASK

- Where do I go for help?
- Is there parent involvement or support?
- How do I keep a grade book?
- How do I deal with behavior problems? Where do I obtain strategies?
- How do I serve the needs of diverse learners?
- What should my literacy block look like?
- What are the school procedures, routines, and policies with which I need to be familiar? (Where do I pick the students up? How do I dispose of boxes or large garbage? Where do I go for art supplies? How do I learn about policies for recess, restroom use, lunch, tardiness, late work, report cards, progress reports, conferences, duties, fire and tornado drills, a sick or hurt child, etc.)
- Should I review records?
- How do I manage time with lessons and units?
- What does a realistic and effective lesson plan for the first week of school look like?
- What will I be evaluated on?
- How do I work with confrontational parents?
- How do I work with gray-area students who don't qualify for special education?
- Are there guidelines for basal and teacher-made units?
- Where do I obtain support for the at-risk students?
- Is my job secure?

- Do I have a budget? How do I pay for things?
- How do I refer a student?
- Where do I get supplies?
- What am I supposed to teach? Where is the curriculum housed?
- How are policies enforced and by whom?
- What are the standards for teaching and learning?
- How do I relate to administration?
- What types of things can I ask office staff to do?
- Who will allow me to vent without discussing my comments?
- How do I demonstrate confidence?
- How should I physically set up my room?
- Is there communication and support among teachers? Administrators and teachers?
- How do I earn the respect of the students? Parents? Colleagues?
- How do I get them to like me?
- How do parents view me? Too tough? Too easy? Involved?
- Are there team planning opportunities?
- How do I gain control of the classroom?
- How do I bridge the gap between best practice and survival?
- How do I work with cultural differences?
- Do we recycle?
- What do I need to know about tax information? Housing allowances? Mileage/gas reimbursement?
- Is there schoolwide discipline in place? How does detention work?

- How does the lunch program work?
- How do I overcome being nervous?
- What types of student support services are available?
- Who's responsible for what?
- How do we tie into the high school?
- How do I learn students' abilities as well as learning styles?
- How do I manage time?
- How do I meet the special needs of my students?
- How do I communicate with parents?
- What types of home lives am I dealing with, and what resources are available to students?
- What are the behavioral and academic needs of my students?
- Do we conduct home visits? What are the expectations and procedures for them?
- What do I need to know about the school budget?
- How do I deal with split classrooms?
- What are the staff relations like?
- Am I prepared to teach what I was hired for?
- How do I assess needs at the beginning of the year?
- How do I deal with being hired late with little to no set-up time?

WHAT NEW TEACHERS WANT

- Feedback from the principal and colleagues
- Strategies for classroom management
- Hands-on assessment tools

- Resources for at-risk or gray-area students
- Materials and supplies
- Curriculum
- Support
- A manual of "who's who" at the school and within the district
- One resource area to prepare a package for new staff with a parent handbook, staff directory, etc. so they don't have to be hunted down
- A calendar of events
- A tour of the school
- A detailed map of the school premises
- An orientation session for faculty new to the school
- A mentor
- To provide structure within the classroom
- To handle a large workload
- To reach the necessary standards by the end of the year

ADVICE FOR NEW TEACHERS

- Understand the politics you're dealing with.
- Get to know the policies you're responsible for enforcing.
- Set personal and professional goals.
- Use your colleagues.
- Know your material.
- Kids love attention and caring people.
- Listen!

- Be confident.
- Focus on the good days.
- Get involved.
- The first days set the tone for the year.
- You're on your own.
- Keep a positive attitude and an open mind.
- Be flexible.
- Be prepared to make mistakes and learn from them.
- Seek answers.
- Ask questions of your mentor.
- Have someone to provide support and give good advice.
- Put in extra time.
- Dress professionally.
- Use other teachers as a resource.
- Admit if you don't know something.
- Meet deadlines.
- Understand your students (background, history, needs).
- Don't be cliquey or align yourself with one group.
- Don't overextend yourself or volunteer for too many things.

WHAT EVERY NEW TEACHER SHOULD KNOW

Develop Your Own Teaching Style

- Establish your own standards and expectations.
- Get students' attention before giving instructions. Learn their names quickly.

- Get students on task.
- Give clear and specific directions.
- Set realistic timelines for tasks.
- Circulate among students while they're working and make appropriate constructive comments.
- Adapt your teaching style to the level and type of student; it will differ with individual students and classes.
- Be flexible and continue to grow as a teacher.
- Try various approaches; reflect on what does and doesn't work. Consider why.
- Use questioning techniques; move toward more complex levels of questioning when student ability and maturity warrant.
- Avoid teachers' lounge, parking lot, and athletic event negativity.

Prepare Your Classroom

There's a lot of excitement and anticipation (and perhaps a little anxiety) when you finally have a classroom of your own. The preparations will most likely begin the summer prior to your fall teaching assignment. Here are some tips for your classroom:

- Cover all bulletin boards unless prohibited by fire codes. Use different materials, including butcher-block paper, construction paper, fabric, newspaper, or wrapping paper. Most should change throughout the year unless you have one board identified for upcoming events, school news, or other headings that would most likely not change. But the information within the board will still need to be updated. Remember that bulletin boards should reflect the curriculum taught, and students love interactive bulletin boards. Students love to see their work in the spotlight, so try to have a piece from each student at some point in the quarter, semester, or year depending on the bulletin board.

- Avoid clutter. You might know where things are, but it can be distracting or overwhelming to students and doesn't present a very organized appearance to others entering your classroom.

- Check out your storage. Look at the closet, drawers, cupboards, and other nooks and crannies available. Decide the best layout for your classroom, and then begin to organize from there. Plastic containers, baskets, stackable bins, nets, or cardboard storage units can be useful for storing larger items. Smaller items can be kept in shoeboxes, kitchen cutlery trays, spice racks, ice cube trays, or plastic bowls with lids. Many magnetic products can attach to a chalkboard, desk or other metal surface. You might want to consider a pegboard on which to hang hooks, holders, and even little drawers.

- Hang items from the ceiling. Mobiles and other projects are great to view hanging, where they can easily flow and move about. Hooks are often available, with some snapping over existing rails so to be less invasive. However, you want to check with your building administrator prior to hanging items due to security systems and fire codes.

- Be sure to locate normal office items such as scotch tape, paper clips, tissues, stapler (staples and staple remover), rubber bands, chalk and dry erase markers.

- Do you need to reuse a poster, chart, or map that you've used for a lesson? To save your instructional materials, use a piece of laminate, clip it over the item, and use your erasable marker just as if it were on an overhead.

- Are you thinking of a classroom pet? Consider that taking care of a pet is quite a responsibility. Also consider allergies and the personal preferences of your students (some students might be terrified of animals, while others will be very comfortable around them). Animals can teach many life lessons, increase vocabulary, or act as the center of a creative writing activity.

Create a Peaceful School Environment

To have a lasting effect on the school environment, an antiviolence campaign should demonstrate schoolwide commitment to training in and enforcing the campaign, build relationships between faculty and students as well as students themselves, emphasize prosocial behaviors such as sharing and helping, allow the students a voice in school decision-making, and allow students to express themselves without penalty or judgment, openly discuss safety procedures, and work with community and family agencies.

Establish Routine

Routines are procedures that ensure effective use of time and space. Provide an explanation of the routine and then practice it with the students. By dedicating a few hours at the beginning of the year to establishing and practicing routines, you'll avoid repetition and save time in the long run. Prior to the start of school, you'll want to begin thinking about the who, what, when, where, and why of the classroom. Routines can be put in place for:

- Use of the restroom
- Getting necessary supplies from lockers, cubbies, or other parts of the classroom
- Group work
- Transitioning from one activity to another in the classroom
- Dismissal
- Entering the classroom
- Submission of homework
- Submission of late work
- Purchasing a lunch
- Cleaning up
- Acceptable use of a study hall
- Appropriately obtaining the teacher's attention
- Following procedure for academic instruction

- Keeping up with work for portfolios
- Use of special equipment, e.g., science labs, technology, or electronics

Head Off Inappropriate Behavior

- Call the student by name but don't disrupt a lesson to address the behavior. Wait and discuss the problem with the student privately.
- Use eye contact.
- Make sure to praise your students more often than you criticize them.
- Use cues such as the flick of an overhead light, a hand signal, body language, or a short verbal reprimand given at normal speaking tone. Raising one's voice is not a recommended approach of classroom management.
- Stand near the child to improve classroom control (use proximity).
- Tailor consequences to specific individuals and specific actions.
- Keep nonjudgmental, anecdotal records for difficult students to use selectively at conferences and for referrals. Record exactly what happened without interpretation.
- Keep your supervisor informed if a child is a problem. Don't be afraid to ask for help.
- Before contacting a parent about a child's inappropriate behavior, be sure that you can discuss it calmly.

- Show your displeasure at inappropriate behavior without implying that you dislike the child.
- Find something positive about all the children in your classroom, and tell them what it is.
- Don't threaten. Say what you mean and mean what you say.
- Try to handle problems with students before sending them to the office. Reserve that option for major issues.
- Don't argue. Listen, summarize, describe the behavior and how it affects everyone involved, and then give the student the opportunity to alleviate the problem.
- Offer self-instructions to students, such as "*Think* of what you want to say, *raise* your hand, and then *wait* to be called on."
- Openly communicate and collaborate with the student's parent or guardian.
- Remind students that every day offers a fresh start.

Plan Effective Lessons

Effective teachers keep students actively involved in their own learning. If students are engaged, little time is left unaccounted for or wasted during the day, best using the limited amount of time you have with your students. Some strategies to keep students engaged are:

- Have activities for students to do when they enter the classroom or transition between content areas, for example, a journal entry, reflection, chapter summary, problem or puzzle of the day, definitions, or warm-up problems.

- Have materials organized and equipment set up prior to students' arrival.
- Involve all students at some point throughout the lesson.
- Offer a pace that's challenging but not frustrating.
- Prepare additional activities for students who complete work early.
- Determine how and when you'll help students who require additional assistance.

Institute Instructional Strategies

When you choose your instructional strategy, you need to take into account the lesson's objective and assessment as well as the dynamics of that particular class. Some instructional strategies are:

- Expository instruction such as lecture or textbook readings
- Direct instruction
- Mastery learning
- Computer-based instruction
- Online research
- Discovery learning
- In-class activities
- Computer simulators and applications
- Authentic activities

- Teacher questions
- Class discussion
- Reciprocal teaching
- Technology-based discussion
- Cooperative learning
- Peer tutoring
- Homework

Manage Your Time Well

Time management means balancing the different aspects of life. As an adult, you're used to making choices about how you'll spend your time. But take into consideration that your first three years of teaching, your first year in particular, might not be the smoothest. Planning takes additional time because you need to learn new curricula and use new textbooks. You need to spend time writing up teacher resources like games, worksheets, rubrics, and tests, then spend many more hours working out the kinks. In addition, you're learning a new position in a new school, with new faculty and staff, new students, new parents, perhaps even in a new community. Give yourself a good three years to learn your position and become comfortable with your responsibilities.

Time management also includes accurately determining the amount of time lessons will take. New teachers often find they're short of material for their block of teaching time. If you don't know what to do with that time, the students will fill it for you, and it probably won't be educational. Therefore, it's better to have too much material than not enough. As you work with the students, curriculum, and text, you'll become more comfortable and gain better insight into how much time the activities or projects will take.

Plan for the big picture first, and then break the material into smaller units. As you work through your curriculum, your lessons should be tied to state standards (benchmarks or guidelines). Remember that you're responsible for your curriculum, and items like a textbook, computer, or pencil and paper are tools to assist you with instruction. As you become familiar with the standardized tests you need to administer within your content area or grade level, you might want to flip some of your units around to ensure that students receive instruction on specific concepts prior to being tested on them. I'm not saying to "teach to the test"; merely be cognizant of your curriculum and when the students are tested on material. For example, you might choose to teach a unit in October instead of March. The unit hasn't changed; when you teach it has.

Always be certain to meet deadlines, whether for your department, school office, or district. Many times paperwork is necessary for state or federal reports. Be professional and provide the necessary information without requiring that someone chase you down.

Manage Your Classroom Effectively

Effective classroom management creates and maintains a classroom environment that's conducive to learning and achievement. Classroom management techniques *should* vary based on the instructional strategy being used. For example, when engaged in a hands-on activity, the students should have different expectations than when they're engaged in expository instruction.

As a teacher, you need to consider whether you want to have students actively participate in setting classroom rules, which provides ownership and a sense of community, or establishing rules on your own and explaining them to the students. You also need to consider whether you want rules, or guidelines and classroom norms. Determine your approach in working with students when classroom rules are broken. Will outside factors and student diversity be taken into account, and if so, how? What's the best way to assist students in learning appropriate behavior? How do you teach children that not many mistakes are fatal? How do you give students the tools they need to be accountable, learn, and grow from mistakes?

To create and maintain a productive learning environment, effective teachers typically:

- Physically arrange the classroom in a way that minimizes distractions and facilitates teacher–student interaction
- Create a climate in which students feel they belong and are intrinsically motivated to learn
- Set reasonable limits for behavior
- Plan activities that encourage on-task behavior
- Continually monitor what students are doing

- Modify instructional strategies when necessary. (Ormrod, 2006)

- Organize and prepare for each day's teaching. It shows that you enjoy teaching and take your responsibilities as a teacher seriously. Have a written plan to ensure that you've thought the lesson through and have all necessary materials and supplies. How can you expect your students to be prepared for class if you're making it up as you go along, or are scrambling for materials, supplies, or copies as the lesson begins? When you've completed the lesson, be a reflective practitioner and consider what went well as well as what you could have done differently with your lesson. Make notations or keep a journal, particularly during your first year in the classroom.

- The classroom climate, or psychological atmosphere, must allow students to feel safe, secure, willing to make mistakes, and willing to take risks, in an environment of mutual respect and support.

- To get children's attention, use cues such as eye contact, hand signals, and nonthreatening vocal contact.

- Avoid overstimulating students by presenting material and instructions in blocks, and offer only the materials necessary for the current lesson.

- Look over your curriculum at the beginning of the term to establish long-range goals. Be selective and adaptable based on class and student needs. Check and review your decision throughout the year. Make notations in your curriculum for that particular class that can be passed on to the next teacher.

- Assist students in being responsible by announcing upcoming events, projects, assignments, and deadlines. Establish a classroom routine that allows students to keep up with their schoolwork with little day-to-day guidance. Allow students to choose from a list of projects or establish a due date with your assistance.
- Establish good rapport with students, parents, faculty, and staff. If you respect them, they'll respect you.
- Practice specific organizational skills with students. For example, make sure students write down their homework assignments in an assignment book; make sure students go over their tests carefully and don't look at just their grades; and be sure student work goes home and isn't discarded.
- Give immediate and specific feedback if possible.
- Actively interact with every child every day. Humans are social by nature.
- You're responsible for the students in your classroom. Know what they're doing and become familiar with personality traits that might give you insight into whether a student understands material or not, is bored, is acting out or just having a bad day, etc.
- Establish a sense of community so every child feels that he or she belongs and is valued.
- Set reasonable limits on classroom behavior so students understand the expectations and are encouraged to continue to develop and grow. A few rules can be given by the teacher at the beginning of the year in an informative, not controlling, manner.

These rules should be reviewed often at first, occasionally throughout the year, and particularly after longer breaks so students are aware that the expectations have not changed. Enforce the rules in a fair and consistent manner.

- Assist students in evaluating themselves: how they did, what they did right, what they did wrong, what (specifically) they could do to change their behavior.
- Intervene promptly to stop inappropriate behavior.

Maintain a Professional Classroom Demeanor

- Model courtesy, politeness, and mutual respect.
- Use a "quiet" voice in the classroom.
- Be aware that your voice, movements, body language, and attire will be reflected in students' behavior.
- Dress professionally. Think about the image you're portraying.
- Be fair and consistent.

Set Classroom Rules

- Make sure they're consistent with building policies.
- Make them with the cooperation of the students.
- Make them specific.
- See that they're clearly stated.
- Make them reasonable.
- Be sure they're enforceable.
- They should be logically consistent.

- Provide follow-through.
- Post your expectations.
- Keep the list brief; too many "little" rules can be confusing.

Keep in Contact with Parents

- Decide what method of contact is best for the particular situation: personal conference, telephone, mail, note, e-mail. Inquire as to whether parents can receive telephone calls at work and the contact methods preferred.
- Think over what you want to say. Organize your thoughts. Perhaps discuss the situation and what you propose to say and do with your colleague. Focus on the expected result of this contact with the parent. You might want to consult with the principal, your mentor, or a colleague for help and advice.
- Have your information and materials organized. Write down what you'll say.
- Make sure you're calm, collected, and prepared before any type of parental contact.
- Document your contact for your own records.
- Keep your principal informed of these contacts.

Have Parent–Teacher–Student Conferences

- Know when the conferences are scheduled.
- Remind parents of their conference times and express your eagerness to meet.
- Dress professionally.

- Think about what you specifically want to discuss concerning each student, and what work should be shared with the parent. Allow the student a voice in choosing work to share as well as the actual sharing process.
- Start your conference on a positive note.
- Stick to the subject. There really isn't time to talk about personal experience or to stray too far from the purpose of the conference.
- Allow the students to speak — it's an opportunity for them to discuss what's taking place in the classroom, their strengths and weaknesses, and goals.
- Avoid discussing other children.
- Listen to what the parents have to say. To them, their child is unique and deserves to be given individual consideration, just as every other child in your class.
- Be ready not only with suggestions for improvement but with recommendations or procedures that might aid in improvement.
- Before you finish the conference, recap what you, the parents, and the child will do as a result of your discussion. Be sure to give specific suggestions for ways to help the child with schoolwork, and encourage the parents to share their ideas as well.
- If you've agreed to further parent contacts, make sure to follow through.

Set Field Trip Guidelines

The Internet offers many options for virtual tours. While these can be taken in place of field trips, they can also be done prior to the actual visit for students to gain a better understanding of the place and event and ask higher-level questions. Community members are also an excellent resource. The chance to speak with, listen to, and question these community experts gives students a broader perspective of the world outside the classroom. Guest speakers can be great leaders in a field trip experience.

Field trips are an excellent way to bring lessons to life. All students should be able to attend the trip unless there are concerns of safety for the student or the group if the student attends. Have parent–student meetings prior to the trip so expectations are clear and questions can be asked. As the coordinator, you have a huge responsibility and want parents to know that you understand the precious gift in your charge.

When you plan your trip, take into consideration the season and weather typical of the area you plan to visit. Plan well in advance so you have time to put together a nice, enjoyable, and meaningful trip. Mondays aren't typically a good day to plan for a trip. Watch the school calendar for conflicts, such as standardized testing for certain grades, concerts, plays, or athletic events. Once you've decided where and when to go, speak with your principal, department chair, and colleagues to verify there are no conflicts and to invite them to join you. Then you can:

- Officially contact the place you would like to visit. Secure the date and a cost per student. Determine the number of chaperones you'll need. Most establishments will allow a certain number of chaperones for free, and you pay for any beyond that number. If you feel you need additional chaperones, decide if you'll incorporate the cost of the chaperone into the students' overall fee or ask all chaperones to pay a fee that would cover the additional chaperones' entrance.

- Secure transportation for the date and time of your visit, both to and from the establishment. Most trips require bus transportation. Request a proposal from the company so you can incorporate that amount into the overall fee of the field trip. Some field trips could be walking trips and some could require parents or volunteers to drive. There could be special forms for parent drivers due to liability of transporting students in personal vehicles. Transportation in personal vehicles isn't recommended.

- Prepare a field trip permission slip in accordance with the guidelines of your district. Be sure to explicitly state where you'll be going, when, for what purpose (how does it tie into your curriculum?), how long you'll be gone, your return time, and the amount due. Make sure to obtain a parent's signature and date. If the trip extends through the lunch period, state the arrangements. This request should be sent home a few weeks prior to your trip to give you time to follow-up with parents.

- Students aren't allowed to attend without a parental permission slip signed, so you need to make arrangements for any students who cannot go on the trip. If parents don't submit a signed permission slip, it's most likely due to inability to pay, an effort to punish the child, or mistrust of school personnel to take their child off of school grounds. You can contact the parents and discuss the situation. Explain the educational benefit of the trip. If the issue is financial, seek resources (PTA or community group) that might offer assistance, or you might choose to pay for the child yourself.

- Place the field trip on the school's master calendar. Send a reminder to parents approximately one week prior to the trip.
- A few days prior to the trip, you need to finalize arrangements and be sure no last-minute changes have emerged with chaperones, transportation, or establishment.
- Tie the trip to your curriculum. Be sure students understand the connection between the trip and the learning taking place in the classroom. You can create a guidebook, questions, or a study guide for students. Follow-up projects, research, or writing activities can take place. Allow for student feedback when you return from the trip. Make notations as to what students found useful or interesting.
- Be sure to thank your chaperones! Communicating to parents as to how the trip went and what the students viewed and learned is a great follow-up.

Put Suggestions in a Substitute Folder

Keep a separate folder in a location easily accessible by a substitute teacher. At minimum, the folder should include items such as:

- A class list for each class you teach
- Seating chart(s)
- A schedule that includes the times for specialists, lunch, and recess
- Attendance procedures
- Restroom, recess, lunch, and dismissal procedures
- Any duties a substitute will need to undertake on your behalf
- Fire drill, tornado, and other emergency procedures
- Classroom routines, such as where papers should be turned in, how to disburse materials, how the children are grouped for activities, etc.
- The location of lesson plans, worksheets, workbooks, teacher manuals, and any other materials the substitute will need throughout the day
- Any *crucial* student information such as diabetes, asthma, or allergies
- Names and locations of faculty who can answer questions
- Names of at least two responsible students (per class) who can provide assistance throughout the day
- A form letter in which the substitute can provide feedback of material covered and how the day went

Use Internet Resources

Appendix A includes some Internet resources colleagues and I have found particularly helpful. Please note that URLs (addresses) sometimes change, so while this initial list will get you started, you will want to modify, add, or delete information as you work with sites and accumulate your personal favorites.

WORK CITED

Ormrod, J. E. (2006). *Educational Psychology: Developing Learners* (5th ed.). Upper Saddle River, NJ: Pearson Education.

Appendix A

Internet Resources:
Tools to Help You Teach

Note: These sites provide educational opportunities, but many contain advertisements and links to other websites. While the sites offer good, reliable information, I don't take responsibility for the content that's provided, nor the sites' adherence to federal rules to protect children's privacy.

It's important to monitor students' online communication to ensure they don't provide personally identifiable information. You should also preview sites to become familiar with the information, and bookmark or provide specific URLs to deter students from random surfing.

This isn't meant to be a comprehensive list, rather a list of websites to get you started comfortably using and integrating technology into your classroom. Like education itself, educational websites often cannot be pigeonholed into one content area. Therefore, sites are listed by where they *best* fit, but keep an open mind when searching for resources.

REFERENCE AND
HOMEWORK HELPER WEBSITES

Check your state's Department of Public Instruction website. For example, Wisconsin's DPI site is http://www.dpi.state.wi.us and provides such information as state standards, school information, laws, and calendars.

A site of educational resources developed by a team of teachers: http://www.edhelper.com

Educational resources including clip art, lesson plans, and brain boosters: http://school.discovery.com

Tools and resources for the classroom: http://www.teacher.scholastic.com

Educational resources including lesson plans, professional development, and reading strategies : http://education-world.com

This site provides lesson plan ideas, student activities, resources, standards-based web resources, and professional development opportunities: http://www.marcopolo-education.org/home.aspx or http://www.marcopolo-education.org/home.aspz

Lesson plan ideas available by content area: http://www.teachnet.com

Excellent resources, such as lesson plans and rubrics, but many pop-ups and advertisements: http://www.LessonPlans.com

Teacher-tested resources pre-K through adult education: http://ideas.wisconsin.edu

Housed in Florida, this site focuses on reading but provides links to additional teacher resources such as puzzles, rubrics, and quizzes: http://www.sunlink.ucf.edu

An explanation of standards and benchmarks in education: www.mcrel.org/standards-benchmarks/docs/process.asp

This site has received national recognition and offers reference materials, fun facts, and individualized homework assistance: http://www.factmonster.com

Maps, facts, and descriptions of cities and countries around the world, and suggested links to additional resources as well as contact information for asking specific questions: http://www.worldatlas.com

Wikipedia is a free encyclopedia, offering several services from definitions to information on current events. Keep in mind, however, that the information is supplied (and modified) by users and as such isn't 100% reliable: http://www.wikipedia.org

Dictionary, references, grammar, usage, translator, and more: http://thesaurus.reference.com/

Create your own puzzles in minutes! Includes crosswords, word finds, and other popular puzzles: www.puzzlemaker.com

You don't have to re-create the wheel! This site offers many components to use in creating rubrics, as well as personalized rubrics: http://rubistar.4teachers.org/index.php

From field trips to medication release forms, templates to create notes home in English or Spanish: http://casanotes.4teachers.org

Similar to bookmarking your favorite Web pages, this site allows you to go beyond by organizing your sites for you. It also allows you to set up a daily routine and share information with others: http://www.backflip.com

Assists educators with easy WebQuest style activities: http://pinetlibrary.com/index.php

The Internet public library, a public service organization offered by the University of Michigan: http://www.ipl.org/div/news

Kodak photo galleries for viewing, uploading, editing, and saving your personal photos: http://www.ofoto.com

Photo galleries for viewing or purchasing, and ability to upload your personal photos: http://dotphoto.com

Edit photographs from digital images (website originates in England): http://www.photofiltre.com/

Free program for recording and editing sound: http://audacity.sourceforge.net/

Now freeware instead of shareware, this program allows you to grab digital audio from CDs rather than a soundcard, so its sound quality is excellent; make WAVs, MP3s, and more! http://www.audiograbber.com-us.net/

Mac version of program to share photos and video clips: http://mac.com

Locate specific images as needed: http://images.google
.com

Library of Congress "American memory": http://
memory.loc.gov/

Links to additional sites for lesson planning and educational resources: http://pic4learning.com

Schedules for public television, along with resources
and professional development opportunities: http://
www.pbs.org

Search engine: http://www.kartoo.com

Publicly edited Web directory: http://www.dmoz.com

Exemplary practices in teaching Web evaluation:
http://lib.nmsu.edu/staff/susabeck/checs98.html

Guides that children and teenagers can use to find spe-
cialized engines relating to their interests and school
subjects: http://searchability.com/children.htm

K–12 teacher tools and curriculum support: http://
www.bigchalk.com or http://www.proquestk12.com

Teacher guides available for 260 movies (subscription
required): http://www.teachwithmovies.org/

SBC's website of lessons, WebQuests, and information
for teachers and librarians: http://www.kn.pacbell
.com/wired/fil/

Create a Web page to house links, questions, directions, or explanations: http://www.eduhound.com/
hotlist/

Hosted by the Educational Technology Department of
San Diego State University: http://webquest.sdsu
.edu

Focuses on action research projects with students: http://www.hprtec.org

Create notes for homework and class information and post it to the Web in seconds: http://schoolnotes.com

Assists professional educators in planning, managing, and supporting online courses using online tools, resources, colleagues, and support to implement effective learning activities: http://www.tappedin.org

Assists educators in addressing common technology integration questions by providing practical, online resources and activities: http://eduscapes.com/tap/

The Educational Technology Journal published by Jamie McKenzie, EdD: http://www.fno.org/

The George Lucas Educational Foundation hosts Edutopia: The New World of Learning, which includes professional articles, topics of interest, and professional development opportunities: http://www.glef.org

Translation from English to other languages including Spanish at no cost: http://www.freetranslation.com

MULTIPLE AREAS OF LEARNING

From the United Kingdom, this site offers activities for age groups 4–16 in many content areas. Students choose the appropriate age level and the type of content they want to practice, and they're given a selection of activities. There's also a teacher resource page with helpful information and links: http://www.bbc.co.uk/schools/

Innovative teaching materials for teachers, useful and enjoyable resources for students, and advice for parents on how to help their children enjoy learning and excel in school. The site is constantly reviewed for educational relevance by practicing classroom teachers at the elementary, middle, and high school level: http://school.discovery.com

Provides information on the educational television shows that PBS broadcasts. PBS Kids websites include at-home activities, lesson plans, educational guides, and tips for parents and teachers. Also provides activities and games based on their television shows: www.pbskids.org

An award-winning site that offers early childhood resources: http://www.edupuppy.com

Educational material that emphasizes creativity and the pure enjoyment of learning: http://www.enchantedlearning.com/Home.html

A smart place to play—educational games for different subject areas, as well as resources for teachers and parents: http://www.funbrain.com/

An educational center offering drill games to better students' skills: http://www.edu4kids.com/

Games for all subjects. You can also find online stories and activities for children to work on: http://www.primarygames.com/

The Magic School Bus. Provides games, guided tours, simple science, a theme index, and even a site for parents and teachers: http://www.scholastic.com/magicschoolbus/home.htm

Popular fairy tales, nursery rhymes, holiday stories, and interactive stories: http://www.childrenstory.com/

Kid's Education Place, produced by Houghton Mifflin Company, offers children's games and activities in math, reading, language arts, social studies, and more: http://www.eduplace.com/kids/

The site offers more than 800 interactive games and activities for preschool through 6th grade that are fun and easy to use: http://www.funschool.com/

The mission of this user-friendly site is to produce the best educational material, emphasizing creativity and the pure enjoyment of learning. Though free, a user subscription is available to minimize pop-ups and provide printer-friendly versions of material: http://www.enchantedlearning.com/home.html

EARLY CHILDHOOD

http://members.aol.com/a100thday/ideas.html
http://www.kindergartentreehouse.com/hundreddays.html
http://www.kinderhive.net/100.html
http://mrsalphabet.com/100thday.html

MATH

Time math tests that can be completed on the computer, with immediate feedback: http://www.scugog-net.com/room108/MadMath/mmm.htm

Math problems, games, and articles: http://www.nrich .maths.org.uk

Create games, activities, flash cards, scavenger hunts, and more (subscription necessary): http://www.quia .com/dir/math

Multiplication skills—clicking on the correct answer continues the story: http://schoolcentral.com/ willoughby5/

Multiplication activities: http://www.multiplication .com/internet_games.htm

Multiplication baseball: http://www.prongo.com/math/

Site includes some free drill games, and other resources are available with a membership fee: http:// www.edu4kids.com/index.php

A variety of math activities: http://www.aplusmath.com

AAA math: basic math skills, interactive practice, explanations, and challenge games for grades K–8. These interactive exercises and problems contain a series of basic math lessons, a resource that can be used by math students in formal elementary education math classes, home schooling, or elsewhere: http://www.aaamath.com/

Math games and explanations for students from age three through high school: http://www.coolmath .com/home.htm

SCIENCE

This site provides excellent resources for kids, students, and teachers: homework help, Internet resources, multimedia, and contact information for grades K–4, 5–8, and 9–12: http://www.nasa.gov/home/index.html

Grand explanation of the Shedd Aquarium: http://www.sheddnet.org

From science projects to games, these sites have something for all ages: http://www.sandiegozoo and http://www.planetpals.com/weather.html

Dozens of atmospheric, oceanic, geophysical, and space science sites: http://www.cv.nrao.edu/fits/www/yp_earth.html

Yahoo listing of science- and astronomy-related topics: http://www.yahoo.com/Science/Astronomy/

The Howard Hughes Medical Institute invites curious children to explore biology and gain an appreciation of science. Designed to show students in grades K–3 that science is fun, practical, and realistic: http://www.hhmi.org/coolscience/

Jurassic Park's Dinosaur Site, interactive and informational: http://www.jpinstitute.com

Animal Diversity Web is an online database of animal natural history, distribution, classification, and conservation biology at the University of Michigan: http://animaldiversity.ummz.umich.edu/site/index.html

This child-friendly site offers interactive information on careers, animal care, and general information about animals. Very nice graphics. Operated by the American Society for the Prevention of Cruelty to Animals: http://www.animaland.org/

Freddo Frog's Pond on the Web—provides discussion on environmental and safety issues: http://www.greenweb.com.au/freddo/index.html

Comprehensive site about the world of insects, ranging from identification to bug cuisine: http://www.insectclopedia.com/

Defenders of Wildlife is dedicated to the protection of all native wild animals and plants in their natural communities. The programs focus on what scientists consider two of the most serious environmental threats to the planet: the accelerating rate of extinction of species and associated loss of biological diversity, and habitat alteration and destruction: http://www.kidsplanet.org/

National Wildlife Federation is the nation's largest and oldest protector of wildlife. The Kids' Page features articles in English and Spanish from Ranger Rick, an environmental magazine for children; a homework help section; and briefings on issues such as the wetlands, endangered animals, and water quality: http://www.nwf.org/kids/

Tips for taking care of your pet from the American Animal Hospital Association. Lets you find the pet hospital nearest to where you live: http://www.healthypet.com/Library/index.html#caretips

The Sea World/Busch Gardens animal information database is designed especially for students and teachers, bringing the world of wildlife to the classroom! Download cool animal facts, teacher's guides, quizzes, and activities. Even check out live animal cams!: http://www.seaworld.org

SOCIAL STUDIES

Answers questions regarding geography, maps, travel, and flags: http://www.graphicmaps.com/clipart.hrm

A direct link to the Smithsonian Institution, or our "Nation's attic": http://www.si.edu/

Research for pictures, articles, maps, and more. Includes MapMachine to locate a city or country: http://www.nationalgeographic.com/kids/

Pictures and facts about each of our presidents: http://www.americanpresidents.org

Provides information on America's history. Children can play games that have to do with the states and the history of the U.S.: http://www.americaslibrary.gov/cgi.bin/page.cgi

Provides links to federal kids' sites along with some of the best sites from other organizations grouped by subject. This site also has different categories such as arts, careers, computers, geography, health, history, and music. Offers links to other sites: http://www.kids.gov/

Time for Kids Online, offered at levels K, 1, 2, 3, and 4–6. Children can keep up with the news written on their grade level: http://www.timeforkids.com/TFK/

Presidents

http://www.americanpresidents.org
http://www.whitehouse.gov
http://www.presidentsusa.net
http://gi.grolier.com/presidents/

50 States

http://www.theus50.com
http://www.infoplease.com/states.html
http://factfinder.census.gov/home/en/kids/funfacts/fun
    facts.html
http://www.netstate.com/states/index.html
http://www.50states.com

History of Wisconsin

http://www.wisconsin.gov/state/core/wisconsin_state_
    capitol_tour.html
http://www.50states.com/wisconsin.htm
http://www.wisconsinhistory.org/turningpoints/subtopic
    .asp?tid=1
http://agency.travelwisconsin.com/PR/Tourism_Facts/
    Facts.shtm
http://www.infoplease.com/ipa/A0108291.html
http://www.wisconsin.gov/state/core/wisconsin_state_
    capitol_tour.html
http://www.wisconsinhistory.org/turningpoints/subtopic
    .asp?tid=1

LANGUAGE ARTS

http://eleaston.com
www.thepoetsanctuary.net
www.teenwriting.about.com/od/writingpoetry
http://flyingarts.net/workshops/basics/
http://www.shadowpoetry.com/resources/wip/types
    .html
http://www.rhymer.com/

CREATIVITY AND EDUCATIONAL GAMES

A site for children to color, do arts and crafts, play
    games in the game room, make a card for someone,
    do different activities, visit the crayola factory, and
    visit the crayola store: http://www.crayola.com/kids/
This sites offers puzzles, games, and related materials
    designed to stimulate learning, problem solving, and
    creative thinking: http://www.agameday.com
Chess Kids. Learn to play chess with interactive les-
    sons, quizzes, games, and puzzles: http://www
    .chesskids.com
Kid Wizard is a fun, educational place where kids ages
    six to twelve can play games, solve mysteries, make
    decisions in the interactive story, and find out that
    magic does exist: http://www.kidwizard.com/
Kids Hub is a free online interactive learning center for
    elementary school students. It features fun educa-
    tional games, puzzles, and quizzes: http://kidshub
    .org/kids/kids.cfm

Words and sound clips for chosen nursery rhymes and children's songs around the world: http://www.ma-malisa.com/world/

VIRTUAL TOURS

http://www.senate.gov/vtour
http://www.virtualfreesites.com/tours.html
http://www.virtualfreesites.com/us.government.html
http://www.chinavista.com/travel/virtualtours.html
http://www.louvre.fr/llv/commun/home_flash.jsp?
  bmLocale=en
http://archpropplan.auckland.ac.nz/virtualtour/

ART

http://www.edbydesign.com/art/artists.html
http://www.moma.org/destination/
http://www.scituate.k12.ma.us/docent/
www.artlex.com
www.thewaichulisstudio.net
www.metmuseum.org
www.moma.org
www.mam.org

MUSIC

http://www.isd77.k12.mn.us/resources/staffpages/shirk/
  k12.music.html

http://musiced.about.com/
http://www.creatingmusic.com
http://www.sphinxkids.org
http://www.edu-cyberpg.com/Music/m_sites2.html
http://datadragon.com/education/

LISTINGS OF OTHER WEBSITES

An extensive list of educational and fun websites in many different areas of learning: http://www.busy teacherscafe.com/kidsite.htm#General%20Websites

Just for Kids. Provides links to sites about animals, dinosaurs, educational games, "just for fun," magazines and news, science and museums, space, sports, travel, TV, radio and music: http://www.eagle.ca/~matink/kids.html

The Association for Library Service to Children website provides links to educational sites on animals, the arts, history and biographies, literature and language, math and computers, social sciences, and science: http://www.ala.org/ala/alsc/greatwebsites/great websiteskids.htm

The mission of Cyberkids is to provide a voice for young people on the Internet, a place where original creative work by kids ages 7 to 12 can be published: http://www.cyberkids.com/index.html

Appendix B

Parent–Teacher Communication

LETTER 1

August 2006
Dear Parents and Second Grade Students:

Hello! My name is Mrs. Strike, and I will be your teacher for the 2006–2007 school year at Red Apple. This is my 18th year teaching, but every year seems like the first year in some ways because every year is new and different. This year we will be pen pals with a class in North Carolina, and a class in Datong, China. Our class was chosen as one of the three classes in our school to pilot the technology immersion program. This program allows us to have one computer for every two students, plus a local area network, local printer, and network printer right in our classroom! We will also be implementing the new reading series adopted by the district last spring. As you can tell, we have a busy year ahead of us.

As you know, school begins with a half day on Wednesday, August 30. Students will be released at 11:15, and lunch will not be served on that day. This day allows us to bring our school supplies to school and unpack. It also allows us to get to know each other. On Thursday, we will begin our regular classroom routine. As part of this routine, you will find that there are certain things we will do every week. For example, please look for your child's Take Home Folder on Wednesday. This folder holds all communications from the school office as well as specific information from clubs and organizations. The school newsletter and lunch menu will also come home in this folder. I ask that you sign the sheet located within the folder to show that you received and viewed the material. In our classroom, you will receive a classroom newsletter on Fridays. This newsletter will tell you what we have done throughout the last week and provide information about upcoming lessons, projects, and special events. By reading and discussing this sheet with your child, you can reinforce learned skills and share the enthusiasm of our classroom. On Mondays we will have a pretest in spelling. On Fridays we will have a test in both spelling and daily oral usage. Tests in content areas, such as social studies or science, will be announced in the classroom newsletter.

Your child has physical education on Mondays and Thursdays, so please be sure to dress appropriately and wear tennis shoes. Music is on Tuesdays and Fridays and art is on Wednesdays.

Please be sure your child reports to school with the supplies listed. Clearly mark all supplies and personal items such as hats and gloves to avoid mix-ups.

I look forward to meeting you in person!

Sincerely,
Mrs. Strike

LETTER 2

September 2006
Dear Parents:

On Tuesday, September 19, I hope that you can join us at Red Apple School for an open house from 6:00 to 8:00 in the evening. During that time, your child can bring you through our classroom and show you some of his or her work. You will become familiar with our classroom schedule and meet other teachers who work with your child for reading, math, and specialty areas such as art, physical education, and music. The evening is family-oriented, and siblings are welcome. The PTA has special events planned, and you will re-ceive additional information from them as the date grows closer.

While I would like to discuss your child's progress with you, please understand that this open house is not the appropriate forum to do so. If you have concerns, please feel free to contact me via telephone at 555-1212 or e-mail at kstrike@redapple.k12.wi.us to en-sure we have the privacy and time to address your questions or concerns. If I have concerns about your child, I will already have contacted you. Parent–teacher–student conferences will be held November 15–17, and I will be meeting with each of you during this time. I will have a sign-up sheet available at the open house for your convenience.

Your child has created a special project for you and is eager to present it to you. I look forward to meeting you. Please feel free to contact me with any questions.

Sincerely,
Mrs. Strike

LETTER 3

October 2006
Dear Parents:

On Tuesday, October 31, we will hold our annual Halloween party. Students may bring their costumes to school in a bag marked with their name. Costumes may not have weapons and may not be of a violent or gory nature. Masks make it difficult for the child to see or participate in activities, so you might want to explore options without a mask. Students may apply make-up here at school, but hairspray and baby powder are not allowed. We really like to promote creativity in the children. Therefore, you might want to talk to your child about his or her favorite character in a book, movie, or game and see if you can bring it to life! Or perhaps there is an inanimate object that you'd like to tackle. For example, one of the most creative costumes I have seen was a boy painted white with ivy around his head, a toga on his body, and a styrofoam column up to his chest so he looked like a bust on a pillar.

Our room parents are busy planning some events for the day. We will need some additional sets of hands to assist students getting into costumes, serving treats, and playing games. If you are available to help, please contact either Sue Smith at 555-2323 or me at 555-1212.

Thank you,
Mrs. Strike

LETTER 4

November 2006
Dear Parents:

Parent–teacher–student conferences are right around the corner. I am excitedly waiting for the opportunity to discuss your child's progress with you. These conferences allow for a three-way conversation to take place. This is important for several reasons. First, you are your child's best teacher and know your child best. You know your child's strengths and weaknesses. Second, your child is an active participant in this partnership. Without his or her effort and attention, learning would not take place. Therefore, it is important to hear your child's perspective of how things are going, what is working, and what needs work. Finally, I have the privilege of teaching your child this year. For us to best use our short time together, I have a few questions I would like you to answer. By returning the completed sheet prior to the conference, it will allow me to see if you have specific questions or concerns and gather additional information for you. I have attached the sheet for your convenience.

Your conference time is scheduled for 3:20–3:40 on Thursday, November 16. You child is the STAR! Please be sure he or she attends with you. Arrangements should be made for siblings. I will have an activity table set up in the hallway for children to color, read, and build.

If you need to change your appointment, please contact me at 555-1212 to make other arrangements.

I look forward to our meeting,

Mrs. Strike

LETTER 5

December 12, 2006
Dear Parents:

Just a reminder that our Holiday Concert is coming up on Tuesday, December 19. Students should report to their homerooms at 6:45. The concert will begin at 7:00, and last approximately 1.5 hours. Attire is dark pants and a light shirt, or attire that reflects the holiday spirit. We hope that you will join us for this special event.

Happy Holidays!

Mrs. Strike

CONFERENCE QUESTIONS

1. What my child likes best about school is:

_____

_____

_____

2. What my child likes least about school is:

_____

_____

_____

3. One question I'd really like to ask is:

_____

_____

_____

4. Four words I would use to describe my child are:

_____

_____

_____

5. Four words my child uses to describe him or herself are:

_____

_____

_____

FROM THE DESK OF _____
WEEK OF _____

Language Arts:

_____

_____

_____

Mathematics:

_____

_____

_____

Science and Health:

_____

_____

_____

Social Studies:

_____

_____

_____

Special Events:

_____

_____

_____

Upcoming Projects or Events:

_____

_____

_____

Missing Work and/or Concerns:

_____

_____

_____

BEHAVIOR REPORT FOR _____

Date: _____

Subject	How I Think I Did	How the Teacher Thinks I Did
Reading		
Math		
Specialist		

Parent Signature: _____

PROGRESS REPORT FOR _____

Date: _____

Task	Yes	No
I raised my hand to speak		
I stayed in my seat		
I remained on task		
I completed my work (well done and on time)		
I was a good listener		

Comments: _____

_____

_____

_____

Missing Work:

_____

_____

_____

Parent Signature:_____

PROGRESS REPORT FOR _____

Date: _____

Class	Teacher comments	Grade	Missing Work	Work Habits in Class
Math				
English				
Spelling/ Vocab.				
Reading/ Lit.				
Soc. Studies				
Science				
Specialist				

Parent Signature: _____

REFERENCES

Diffily, D., and Sessman, C. (2004). *Teaching Effective Classroom Routines.* New York, NY: Scholastic, Inc.

Gavaert, C. (2006). *Using Free Software in the Waukesha Public Schools.* Milwaukee, WI. Milwaukee Educational Computing Association (MECA) newsletter V15 N3 P3.

Learning Books. (1987). *Classroom Management.* Bethlehem Pike, Springfield, PA: Springhouse Corporation.

Ormrod, J. E. (2006). *Educational psychology: Developing learners* (5th ed.). Upper Saddle River, NJ: Pearson Education.

Wisconsin Education Association Council (WEAC). (1989). *The Beginning Teacher Handbook: A Book of Firsts.* Madison, WI. Developed by the WEAC Instruction and Professional Development Committee (IPD).

http://www.competitionmaster.com/pages/career/profes sionalism.html (retrieved 12/27/05).

http://www.goalsinstitute.com/professionalism-g.html ?gclid=CI6_sJWwnYICFQ7hIgodCibuDQ (retrieved 12/27/05).

About the Author

Kimberly T. Strike (doctorate, Marquette University) has been an administrator, teacher, educational consultant, and guest speaker. Her experience crosses public, private, and parochial sectors; urban and rural districts; and adult and youth education. She was an educational ambassador to China (Datong and Beijing) in 2005 and a missionary to Russia (Ivanovo and Moscow) in 2006.